WORLD CUP
COCK UPS!

First published in Great Britain in 1998 by

Chameleon Books

76 Dean Street

London W1V 5HA

Copyright for text © Generation Publications

All rights reserved

CIP data for this title is available from the British Library

ISBN 0 233 99355 X

Book and jacket Design Generation Studio.

Origination by Digicol Link, London.

Printed in Spain.

Andre Deutsch Ltd is a VCI plc company.

ACKNOWLEDGEMENTS:

A special thanks to Dave Crowe, Tim Vigon, Linda Baritski,
Paul Sudbury, (Veronica, Becky, Ellie & Ben), Matthew Sudbury, Mark Peacock.

PHOTOGRAPH ACKNOWLEDGEMENTS

All photographs courtesy of Allsport.

DEDICATED TO:

Alex Wood, Amy Lord, Ollie Wood, Antony Crockett, Sam Hardwick, Marcus Richardson, Dave Hammond, Izzie Norgrove, Ellie Crowe, Joe Crowe Dan Crowe, Jonty French, Simon French, Ali Smee, Chris Marrot, Dan "Ghandi" Baker, Robbie Orten, Nick England, Fran and Henrey Hodgetts, Binny Collins, Tav Douglas, Jamie Bruice, Jamie Berienger, Cez, Vicky and John Lord, Phil Carter, Lucy Godwin, Jonney Valentine and The Huggins .

"For all its commercial pomp and circumstance, the World Cup is not just a showcase for the best football the world has to offer - it's also an exercise in international relations and a microcosm of the global game complete with all its foibles and eccentricities (both on and off the pitch). It's also probably the only time even your gran takes an interest in the game. The truth is that for every golden World Cup moment such as Michael Owen's superb strike against Argentina, there are a dozen shameful tackles, a clutch of dodgy refereeing decisions and a 'hand'ful of major injustices. But the uncertainty (unless you're a Scotland fan) is part of the excitement of the World Cup and this book celebrates the less than great moments in World Cup history - the moments that make team mates hold their heads in despair, managers turn to faith healers and the fans drop off to sleep.

It's a funny old game..."

Trevor Brooking

CHAPTER ONE
WORLD CUP WINNERS

"Quick. Just take the picture. It's not like any one's ever going to see it, is it?"

It's the ultimate prize in football. Lifting the World Cup is the dream of every footballer from the East Lancashire Sunday League to Serie A, and only a precious few actually get their hands on it. Winning the World Cup sets you up for life. Just ask any of England's 1966 heroes who can still charge silly money to tell their tales on the after dinner circuit. But when you think that only eleven British people ever have been in a World Cup winning team, it tells you just what it means to those who have made it.

Since the competition began in 1930 there have been fifteen tournaments. In this time only seven teams have won it, and between 1970 and 1994, five teams (Germany, Italy, Brazil, Argentina and Holland) had the final to themselves . History tells us that in the World Cup, winners are few and losers are many, but in a tournament with as much exposure and importance as this, everyone has a story to tell - this chapter looks at the funny things that have happened on the way to victory.

URUGUAY - ARMLESS?

Despite winning the inaugural tournament, Uruguay must have been the unhappiest World Cup winners in history. They were chosen to host the event ahead of a clutch of European teams when they pledged to pay the expenses of all the visting squads and to build a brand new stadium especially for the competition. The Europeans duly sulked and refused to come (it took three weeks to get there by boat in those days) and even though they went on to win the Cup, the Uruguayans refused to defend it in 1934 or to travel to France in 1938.

The biggest scandal of the 1930 tournament was the match ball debacle in the final itself. Both teams insisted on playing with a ball manufactured in their own country, so the referee had to use a different one in each half! Unsurprisingly, no one asked Uruguay's Cup Final goalscorer Hector Castro if he needed a hand, as he had lost his left one in a childhood accident!

Ironically the Uruguayans won the trophy for the second and final time on their return to the tournament in 1950. Which must make them feel a bit daft for missing out on the ones in between!

ITALY - DIPS NO FLUKE - OH ALL RIGHT THEN IT IS!

The Italians have a fine World Cup legacy and boast a win at all costs reputation. They hosted the tournament in 1934 and duly won it. The benefactor was one Benito Mussolini whose fascist government footed the bill, he was insistent that his Italian team were "world beaters" (despite the inclusion of a number of players poached from other countries!). His attitude was a taste of things to come although he found his army to be strictly Vauxhall Conference material in the 1940s!

The Italians were actually a goal down in the 1934 final until Argentinian winger Orsi scored with a phenomenal dipping and curling shot. The following day he attended a press call at which he was to show how he had managed to put such a wicked dip on the ball. After 20 failed attempts at an empty net he admitted defeat.

OOPS!

The Italians retained the Cup in France in 1938, becoming the first team to win the trophy on foreign soil. Their semi-final was against the ultra-confident Brazilians and it became a bit of a grudge match. At one-nil, the Italians were awarded a penalty which was converted by their skipper Meazza. In a typical display of Italian style, Meazza turned to celebrate and his ripped shorts fell immediately to his ankles. Talk about spoiling the moment.

It was 44 years before the Italians again lifted the World Cup. Their triumph in Spain in 1982 was strange and unexpected in some ways. Despite a fairly kind draw, they failed to win any of their first round matches against Peru, Cameroon and Poland, scoring only two goals in the process. They qualified at the expense of also unbeaten Cameroon, who had scored only once. Would the mighty Cameroon have gone on to win the World Cup? We'll never know.

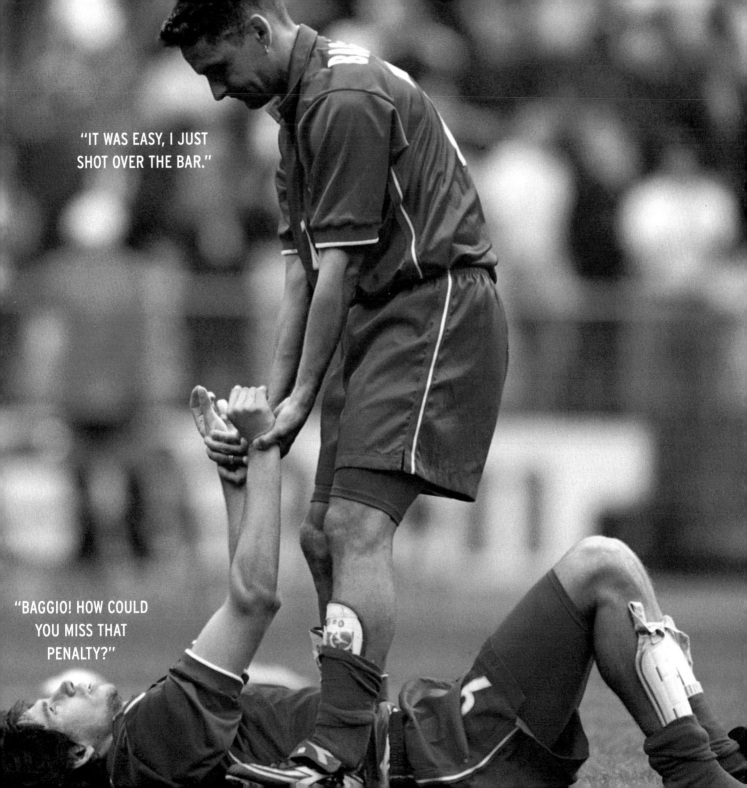

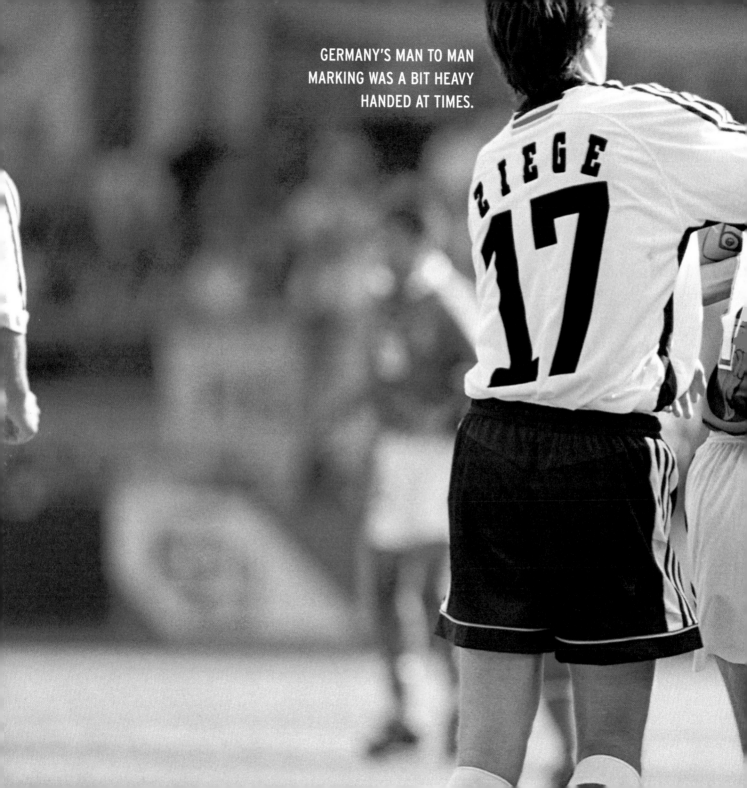

GERMANY'S MAN TO MAN
MARKING WAS A BIT HEAVY
HANDED AT TIMES.

GERMANY - WE HAVE WAYS OF STOPPING YOU WALK

The German's first World Cup victory in Switzerland in 1954 was completely unexpected. The hot favourites were Hungary, clearly the world's greatest team. Their captain, the legendary Ferenc Puskas terrorised defenders and goalkeepers and possessed possibly the greatest left foot in soccer history. Never let it be said that the Germans were cynical in their quest for glory, but in the first game of the tournament, Puskas faced a strapping centre half in Werner Liebrich. Puskas lasted 30 minutes before being carried off with an ankle injury. Although Hungary won the game easily, they were seriously handicapped without their star player and despite his return in the final against the Germans, he was clearly still injured. Germany scraped a 3-2 victory and Liebrich was undoubtably the toast of the German dressing room.

Germany's third World Cup win came at Italy in 1990. They have the dubious honour of competing in what has been tagged "The Worst Final of All Time". Their opponents were Argentina, who were without their star striker Cannigia, suspended for an innocuous handball offence. The usually mercurial Maradona was a shadow of his former self, having picked up a crippling injury, and had made himself public enemy number one with Italian neutrals.

The Argentinians had faced Italy at Napoli (his club side at the time) in the semi-finals, and Maradona had foolishly called for the support of the locals against their national team. The Italians didn't like this and were overjoyed to see a German victory in the final. Two Argentines were dismissed and the Germans won through a penalty that never should have been awarded. Karma ? Maybe so, perhaps the 'hand of god' had returned to blur the referee's vision!

West Germany staged the 1974 tournament, and went on to win it. The final, in Munich's Olympic Stadium was seen by over 800 million television viewers who may have been confused by the lack of corner flags at kick off time. Red faced officials had to correct their mistake in front of the world. This may have harmed the home side's concentration when after 80 seconds of the match they conceded a penalty which Holland converted. At this point Germany had not touched the ball once.

WELL, EVERYONE
THINKS THEY CAN
WALK ON WATER, SO
WHY NOT TRY TO FLY?

BRAZIL - SAMBA STYLE

Brazil have now won the World Cup four times. They were given the original Jules Rimet Trophy after their third victory in Mexico '70 and it is fair to say that they are as much a part of the World Cup as the trophy itself. Everybody watches the progress of the Brazilians and marvels.

Their first victory came in Sweden in 1958, where Brazil became the first team to win the trophy outside of their continent. Coincidentally it was also the tournament which introduced Pele to the world stage. After Pele retired from international football after Mexico in 1970, the Brazilians didn't win the trophy for another 24 years. Is it also a coincidence that 1994 was the first time Ronaldo was included in the Brazilian squad?

The Brazilians hold many world cup records: Youngest goalscorer (Pele aged 17), the only team to appear in all 15 finals, 13 games undefeated between 1958 and 1966, least number of players used to win the tournament (12 in 1962), the list goes on and on.

Brazil retained their trophy in 1962 in Chile despite an early injury to Pele, and after their hiccup in 1966 won back the trophy in Mexico in 1970 with perhaps the greatest team ever to win the World Cup. The USA in 1994 was the first time that the Brazilians managed to get their hands on the new trophy. However, it is unlikely that even if they win this one ten times they will be allowed to keep it. The original Jules Rimet Trophy was stolen in 1983 and is thought to have been melted down!

ENGLAND – "TWO WORLD WARS AND ONE WORLD CUP"

I t is a matter of much frustration in England that the national team has won only one major tournament. Winning the World Cup on home soil in 1966 has become a millstone around the neck of England teams since. Strangely, despite being the host nation, no-one really expected England to come out on top, apart from their manager Sir Alf Ramsey who confidently predicted a home victory before the tournament.

NOTHING LIKE A BIT OF SOLIDARITY AFTER A DEFEAT

SUCKER

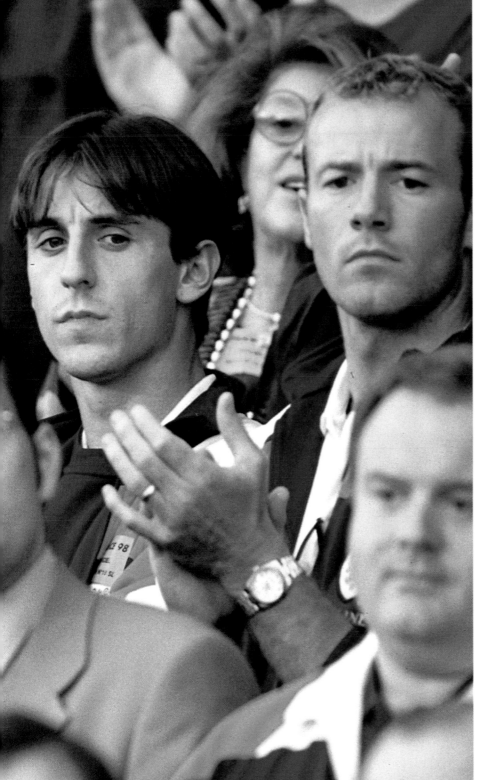

Ramsey, like many England managers since, found his selection policy under increasing criticism as the tournament went on. When the squad was announced, many journalists questioned the omission of Chelsea striker Peter Osgood. His replacement in the squad? A certain Geoff Hurst. Next came the question of Jimmy Greaves, the Michael Owen of the time, who found himself on the bench in the latter stages of the tournament. His replacement was again Mr Hurst - who went on to score the first, and still only, World Cup Final hat trick.

Amazingly, England only had a prize to lift thanks to a dog named Pickles. The Jules Rimet Trophy was stolen from a shop in London where it was on display. Despite a nationwide search it was nowhere to be found until Pickles found it in a hedge wrapped in a copy of the *News of the World*. He was rewarded with a years supply of dog food!

B-ARGENTINA

Argentina had been bidding to stage the tournament ever since the competition began, and when they were finally given the nod in 1978 it was a major achievement for the nation. So important was it, that the military government put a series of advertisments on TV begging the people of Argentina to behave, making sure that the "sunny side" of Argentina was on show to the world.

Argentina and Brazil both qualified for the second stage and were drawn in the same group. The winners were eventually decided on goal difference as Argentina crushed Peru 6-0. There were accusations of bribery and it turned out that the Peruvian keeper was actually born in Argentina. But any wrongdoing was strenuously denied.

ANOTHER HAND OF GOD, DIEGO?

ARE YOU SURE YOU HAD
BOTH OF THEM WHEN YOU
STARTED THE GAME?

Argentina beat Holland 3-1 in the final. But only after some dodgy gamesmanship. They kept the Dutch waiting for 5 minutes before emerging late onto the pitch and then complained about a bandage which the Dutch winger Van Der Kerkhof had worn for the whole of the tournament. Many claim that the Argentines would not have even passed the first stage had the competition been in any other country.

The Argentinian's second World Cup victory came in 1986 when Diego Maradona was at his peak. Speaking of peaks, the manager for that tournament was one Carlos Bilardo, cruelly nicknamed "Bignose" by the Argentinians. Upon returning home following their victory he was greeted by banners proclaiming "Sorry, Bignose, and Thanks"!

DIEGO, EVERYONE'S FAVOURITE ARGENTINIAN.

"I CAN'T LOOK, HAS DIEGO STILL GOT THAT KEVIN KEEGAN PERM?"

"WASN'T IT ABSOLUTELY WONDERFUL TO SEE THE MARVELLOUS, KIND, POLITE, SINCERE, AND MODEST FRENCH WIN THE WORLD CUP?"

FRANCE - VIVE LA REVOLUTION

France became the first 'new' winners of the trophy since Argentina in 1978 with their victory over Brazil. Winning the tournament at home sparked the greatest scenes over the channel since the French revolution, but until the day of the final the players claimed that their support had been somewhat muted. The French are not reknowned for fanatical football support. In fact some of the World Cup matches were played in rugby stadiums.

The French press were not that confident either, roundly criticising the team for lack of firepower (a valid argument in the case of their strikers who only managed 2 goals between them in the whole tournament) and even whilst the French were making their way to their glorious victory, coach Aime Jacquet was arming himself for a hostile attack. It is said that for each match he carried a pile of handwritten notes, not containing tactics, but outlining his reasons for picking the team he had picked in preparation for criticism from the media!

TO A MANCHESTER CITY
FAN THIS WAS THE BEST
PART OF THE WORLD
CUP...

...AND IAN WRIGHT,
ARSENAL FANS, AND
PROBABLY MOST OF THE
PREMIERSHIP.

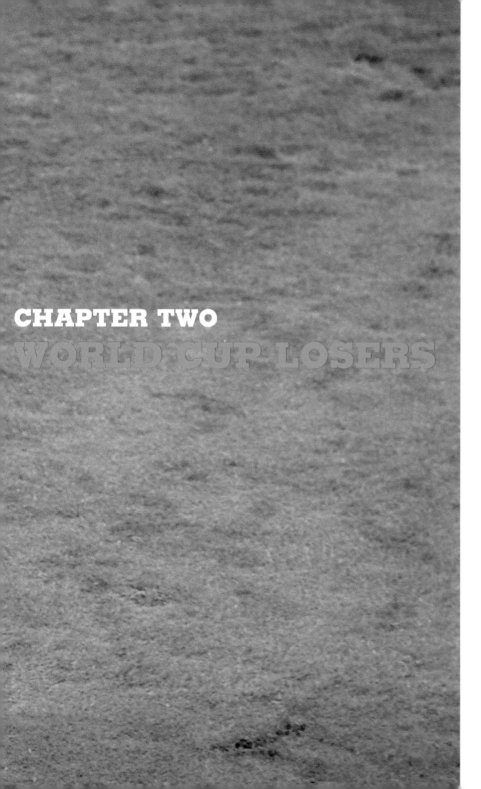

CHAPTER TWO
WORLD CUP LOSERS

144 teams entered the 1994 World Cup. Only Brazil would go on to win. That's 143 losers. Oh Dear. Many teams have made a reputation out of being World Cup losers. Take the Scots, who always manage to qualify and always end up beaten by a supposedly inferior side. Look at the Dutch masters, tagged the greatest team never to win the World Cup. On the other side of the coin there's teams like Cameroon, who despite defeat, have surprised the world with their progress and have returned to their native country as conquering heroes. Losing can affect people in the most strange and extreme manner; this chapter has a look at some of the tournament's most prominent tales of submission.

IT'S ONLY A GAME

Sometimes the disappointment is too much. In 1930, when Argentina lost to Uruguay in the maiden final, the Uruguayan Consulate in Buenos Aires was forced to barricade its doors and take shelter as an angry mob stoned the building! Do we see a pattern emerging here?

ALL THIS WAY FOR NOTHING

Brazil and Argentina have not always had the success of recent times. Indeed in the 1934 tournament in Italy, the South American teams travelled 8000 miles, a difficult journey at that time, to play just 90 minutes of football, being knocked out by Spain and Sweden respectively.

GREEK TRAGEDY

In the early days, participating countries each played only one qualifying match to decide who went to the finals. Poor old Greece drew the imminent champions Italy in 1934 and in 1938 came out of the hat with Hungary, the pre-tournament favourites and eventual finalists.

TURNIP THE TOWN RED

Poor old Graham Taylor. As the man charged with leading England to the 1994 finals he had a tough old time. He baffled the country and the media with some of his selections and when results went against him, one national newspaper decided that he had a head that resembled a turnip. This was a tag that he was unable to get rid of, especially as a much celebrated illustration of "old turnip head" was repeatedly printed.

Taylor's biggest cock up, however, was to allow a TV documentary to be made of England's bid for qualification. This was a terrible miscalculation as the team were to fail miserably, with Taylor's classic performance as a man out of his depth becoming a national joke. Most memorable was his reaction to Norway's first goal in Oslo - "Do I Not Like That" - which ensured a place for Taylor in football's comic history.

AL POMODORO

Italian fans proved that they have their own way of showing disgust at defeat. When the Italian squad of 1966 returned home after their famous defeat by North Korea they were greeted by a shower of the finest home made tomatoes just like Mama used to use.

BIGMOUTH STRIKES AGAIN

Brazil 1950. In the deciding match of the tournament, the host nation face Uruguay needing only a draw to secure the trophy. The Governor of The State of Rio decided to make an official public address before the game. His words were hardly prophetic; "You Brazilians, whom I consider victors of the tournament, you players who in less than a few hours will be crowned champions, you who have no equals in the terrestrial hemisphere, you who are so superior to every other competitor, you whom I already salute as conquerors". The result? Brazil 1 Uruguay 2. A specially composed song "Brazil The Victors" remains unheard to this day.

LEAVE IT OUT!

Brazil's 1938 campaign was wrecked by the strange and ever-so slightly presumptuous behaviour of their coach Adhemar Pimentha. The Brazilians' star striker Leonidas had an incredible scoring record. He equalled a World Record by scoring in his first 10 internationals, and despite a lengthy absence from the side, scored a hat-trick on his return in the first round match v Poland. His scoring continued in the quarter finals against Czechoslovakia which would surely earn him a place in the semi-final line up to face the holders Italy, with their well reknowned high quality defence. No. Leonidas was dropped for the match, the manager claiming he was saving the striker for the final. Brazil lost 2-1

BURN, BABY BURN

It's not always been an easy ride for Brazilian managers. Indeed the Brazilian fans in 1978 showed their displeasure at team boss Claudio Coutinho by burning an effigy of him in the streets! Seems Graham Taylor got off a little lightly.

Paul Gascoigne is undoubtedly a man with the PR skills to match Sadam Hussein's diplomatic skills. In 1990, after winning the hearts of the nation with his talent and tears in Italia '90, he returned home wearing what can only be described as a pair of plastic comedy breasts. A taste of things to come surely, as when playing for the Lazio club in Rome his answer to a match-related question from one of the country's most respected journalists was to burp into the microphone, on national TV. But it doesn't end here, just before England's vital qualifying match with Norway in 1990 he was asked if he had a message for the people of Norway. His reply was succinct - "Yes I do - F*%K Off, Norway". Cheers, Paul. But who can forget perhaps the final straw in Gascoigne's World Cup career. After months out of the game with injury and a large question mark over his fitness, Gazza was pictured out with his mates Rod Stewart, Danny Baker and Chris Evans, blind drunk and eating a greasy Doner Kebab. Genius.

GIN-NO-LA

Tottenham midfielder David Ginola's international career ended tragically during a World Cup Qualifier in 1994. Against Bulgaria in Paris, the French needed only a draw to go through to their first finals since 1986. Ginola was brought on with about 20 minutes to go and was told to keep possession thus using up valuable seconds on the clock. In the final minute, with the score at 1-1, he earned the side a free kick. Instead of playing a simple ball to a team mate, Ginola inexplicably whacked the ball across the area, finding a Bulgarian defender. The Bulgarians broke away and scored the winning goal, knocking the French out of the competition. France's manager at the time, Houllier, (now joint coach at Liverpool) had few words of encouragement for the shattered Ginola: "David Ginola is a criminal, I repeat, a criminal" he said charitably.

A SIGHT, SADLY NOT AS RARE AS THE LOCH NESS MONSTER.

"THE JAPANESE TEAM ADOPTED A STANDING START FOR THE RACE TO THE FIRST FLIGHT HOME".

MACLEOD - CUCKOO LAND

Scotland's campaign in Argentina in 1978 was illuminated by the vivacious coach Ally MacLeod. He had made the mistake of claiming to the media that Scotland could come home with medals. They were knocked out in the first round, following a defeat by Cuba and a dismal draw with Iran. To top all this, Willie Johnston was sent home following a dope test and the Scots were eliminated only on goal difference after defeating eventual finalists Holland 3-1. At his final press conference MacLeod was a dismal figure. As he faced reporters a mongrel dog came and sat with him. MacLeod remarked "Look at me now, not a friend in the world only this mongrel dog". He bent down to stroke the dog and was promptly bitten.

RONAL-DOH!!!

Surely the most bizarre incident during France '98 was the Ronaldo fiasco on the day of the final versus France. The world's most famous player, who was tipped for the Golden Boot and expected to blast his side to victory, nearly didn't play, and he might as well have stayed in bed. There are many different accounts of the day's events, but the most repeated is as follows.

Ronaldo had been feeling the pressure of the biggest match of his life. Despite having played on the continent since the age of 17 and actually going along to the USA as part of the 1994 squad, it was all too much for the tender Brazilian. He also was suffering from a knee injury and was given some painkilling medication. At around 2pm his roommate Roberto Carlos was woken by a choking Ronaldo undergoing some kind of fit. The panicking Carlos screamed for help and unfortunately alerted the whole of the squad who were incredibly shaken by the sight of their star player doing a fine impression of a human vibrator.

Ronaldo was rushed to hospital for tests where thankfully he recovered. Despite having been through possibly a key trauma in his life, his selection became doubtful for the big match. Edmundo (whose nickname is The Animal), his replacement in the team, thought that he was going to play in the World Cup Final. He was wrong. For whatever reason, the Brazilian coach Zagallo decided to use Ronaldo. This last minute decision caused incredible confusion and speculation as the official teamsheet handed in to the referee had Ronaldo as a substitute and Edmundo on the pitch. The world's media went insane, only to be told after 30 minutes of frenetic activity that this was a mistake and Ronaldo would start.

The Brazilians, however, had not been out to warm up. Something was obviously wrong and it is said that on being told of his exclusion from the eleven, Edmundo, the calm, unselfish character that he is, had started a fight with at least 13 members of the squad. Whatever the truth is, it is safe to say that it was not the most settled dressing room in World Cup History. Brazil were rolled over 3-0 by France and looked a shade of the team that had got them that far. Ronaldo did not win the golden boot.

"STOP LOOKING AT MY GIRLFRIEND."

"OUTA MY WAY, THE SIMPSONS ARE ON."

GETTING STONED

Argentina finished bottom of their group in Sweden in 1958, losing to Czechoslovakia and West Germany, beating only little Northern Ireland on the way. As usual, the Argentines proved to be gracious in defeat. On their return home they were bombarded with stones and bricks by an angry mob, which is only reasonable.

IT'S ONLY A GAME

Surely the most shocking cock-up in World Cup history turned out to be Pablo Escobar's own goal which eliminated Colombia from USA 94. It is rumoured that that goal scuppered a huge gamble by one of Colombia's leading drug baron's and, upon his return home, Escobar was shot dead in the street.

"I'M SURE IT WAS THE
WORLD CUP FINAL
TODAY."

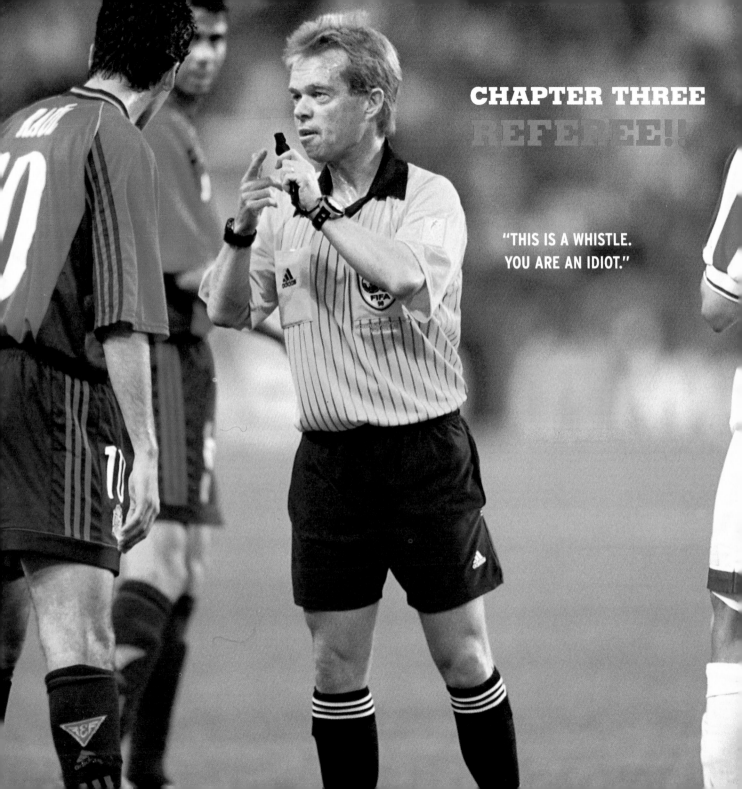

"THIS IS A WHISTLE.
YOU ARE AN IDIOT."

It's an unenviable job being the man in the middle. Whatever you do, someone is always going to be pissed off with you, usually the crowd. On such a giant stage, the World Cup is a great place to make a name for yourself and referees have proved no exception in the quest for fame. Over the years there's been a catalogue of blunders, extravagance and downright showing off. Here's a few of the best.

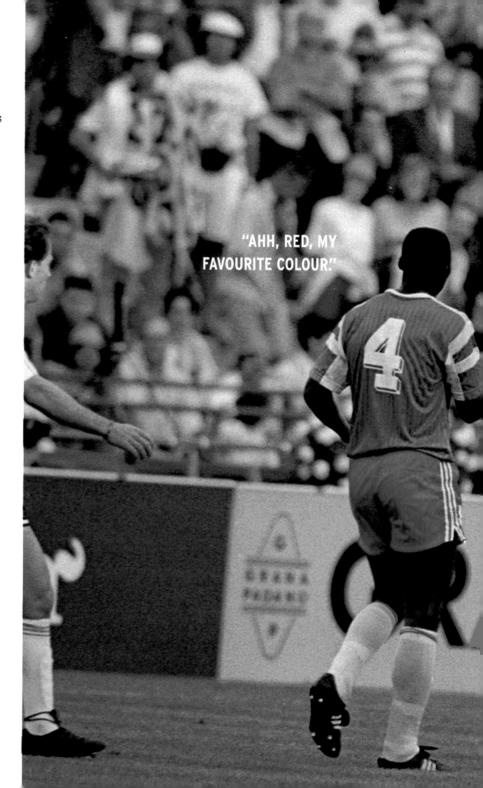

"AHH, RED, MY FAVOURITE COLOUR."

HE'S FINISHED TOO SOON

Almeida Rego of Brazil achieved infamy as the referee for Argentina vs France in the 1930 finals. He blew the final whistle on 84 minutes and caused a huge pitch invasion. The pitch had to be cleared before the players could return and finish the game.

HOW MANY TIMES!

In a match between Chile and Australia in 1974, Australian Raymond Richards was booked twice. The referee didn't put two and two together and Richards was allowed to play on for five minutes until the linesman pointed out that 2 yellows means a sending off!

JUST KU - WAIT

Kuwait's match with France during Spain '82 produced one of the World Cup's most farcical moments. With the score at 3-1 to France, a whistle blew in the crowd which the Kuwait side mistook for the referee. They stopped playing and France ran through to score. A huge row ensued and the Kuwaiti side left the field for over 15 minutes. The country's ruler came down to the pitch and persuaded the team to play again and the referee to disallow the goal!

IT WAS ON THE LINE!!

The biggest controversy of the 1966 final was England's third goal. The game had gone into extra time after a late German equaliser, and with the score at 2-2, Hurst rattled the underside of the crossbar, the ball bounced down over the line - according to the England players - but the Germans were furious. They berated the linesman Mr Bahkramov who instantly pointed to the centre spot - the goal was given. Unsurprisingly, when you talk to Germans and ask them about their 1966 defeat, they claim the key man was the Russian linesman!

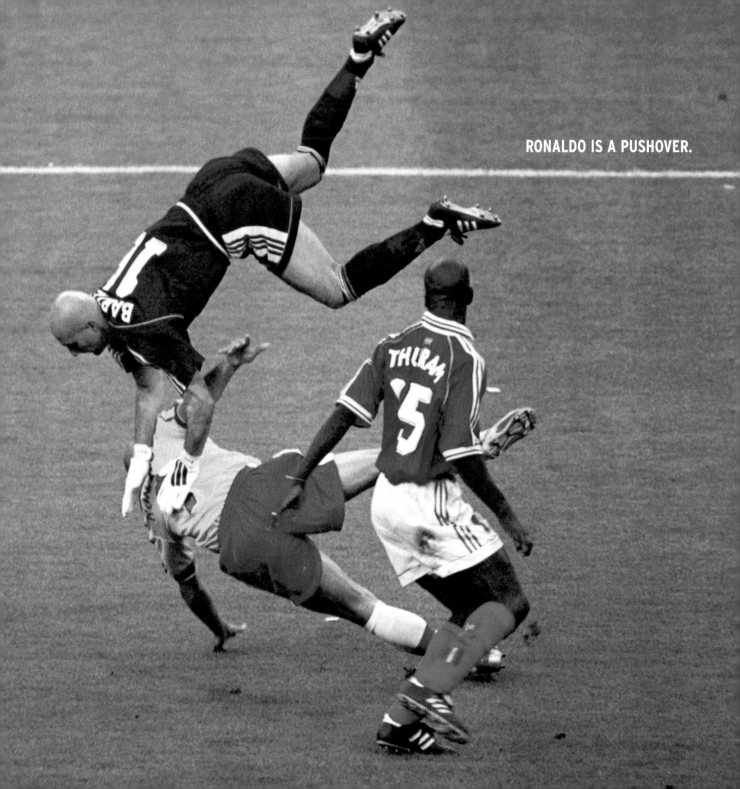

RONALDO IS A PUSHOVER.

"JUST GIVE ME THE BALL AND SHUT IT!"

HE HARDLY TOUCHED HIM!

Everyone who watched the dramatic World Cup Semi-Final between France and West Germany in Spain '82 was shocked and appalled by one of the worst fouls ever committed in the competition - apart from the referee. With the score at 1-1, the French substitute Battiston found himself through on goal with only the German keeper Schumacher to beat. Schumacher dealt with the situation by throwing his full weight at the Frenchman, leading into his face with a forearm, knocking him out cold and taking out two of his teeth at the same time. Amazingly the referee and linesman didn't think the incident warranted any punishment and Schumacher went on to win the match for West Germany in the penalty shootout!

CATCH

England's Ray Wilkins suffered the shame of a sending off against Morocco in 1982 in Spain. His dismissal was even more embarrassing as it was for the rare offence of chucking the ball at the referee - at least he was original!

MEXICAN SAVE

In the match between El Salvador and the hosts Mexico in 1970 there was a bizarre goal scored by the Mexicans following a quickly taken free kick. Of course it's not strange for a free kick to be taken quickly during a football match, but the referee had actually awarded the kick to El Salvador and the Mexicans took it anyway!

"COMING READY OR NOT?"

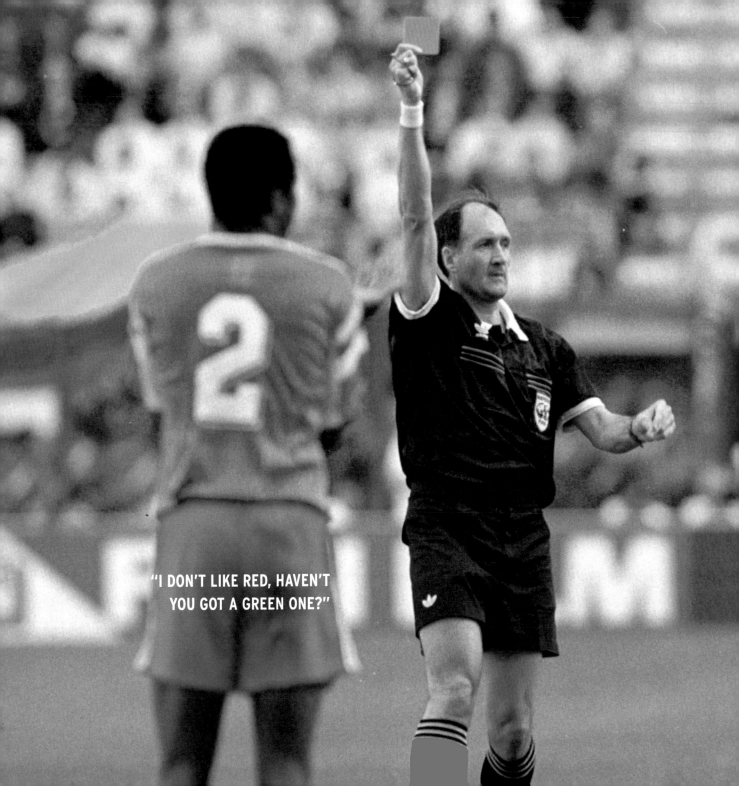

"I DON'T LIKE RED, HAVEN'T YOU GOT A GREEN ONE?"

CHAPTER FOUR

FOUL PLAY

"MY BRAIN HURTS."

SOUTH AMERICAN CHARM

Uruguay's 1966 side was not known for its subtlety. Their match against West Germany in the quarter final was memorable only for the extreme violence of their players. When the Uruguayan captain, Troche, was fouled by a German defender, his response was a kick in the stomach, which didn't go down too well with the referee (or the German). He was sent off, and on his way off he managed to slap the German striker Seeler in the face just for a laugh. Another Uruguayan was sent off for a cynical foul in the second half and there was a close shave for another who 'did a Vinny Jones,' grabbing Helmut Haller where it hurts most and causing him to collapse in agony and urinate blood for the rest of the week. For dessert, another Uruguayan, Cortes, was sent off after the match for kicking the referee!

CALL THE COPS

Discipline in the early days of the World Cup wasn't what it is now. In the 1930 tournament a foul by Argentinian centre-half Monti against Chile caused a massive ruck between players. Without the benefit of TV to incriminate offenders, both teams joined in a full scale ruck, which had to be broken up by police!

FORENSIC EXPERTS LOOKING FOR
DAVID BECKHAM'S BRAIN.

"HEY THAT'S MY PIZZA DELIVERY!"

ARGT 04

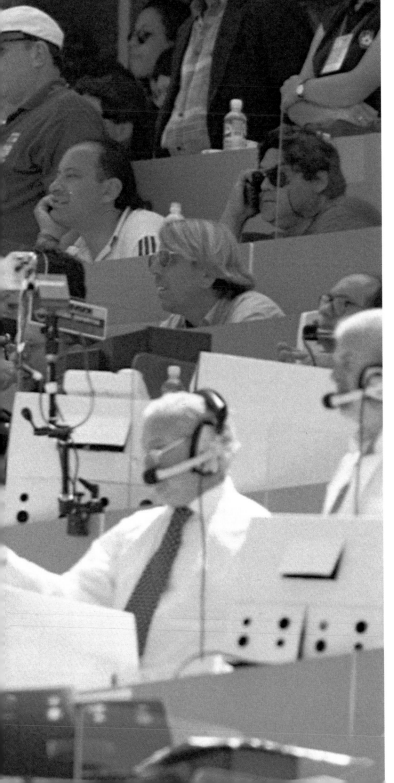

THE BATTLE OF BERNE

English referee Arthur Ellis was at the centre of one of the World Cup's most famous battles. Brazil vs Hungary in the quarter finals in 1954 is notorious for incidents both on and off the pitch. It was a tough and uncompromising match, with much off-the-ball incident and many deliberate fouls on both sides. Tempers obviously frayed and a player from each side was dismissed after a punch-up. This did nothing to curb the violent atmosphere and at one point, one Brazilian player, Djalma Santos, chased the Hungarian striker, Czibor, around the field to try and punch him! Later in the game another Brazilian, Tozzi, was sent off despite begging for forgiveness from Ellis for a terrible foul. It was after the game however that things really turned nasty when the Brazilian squad invaded the Hungarian dressing room and carried on the battle with football boots and bottles. This may or may not have been caused by an alleged attack on the Brazilian centre-half Pinheiro by the injured Ferenc Puskas as the player left the field. Pinheiro needed stitches after being cracked over the head with a glass bottle!

EFFING AND BLINDING

Germany's Steffan Effenberg did himself no favours when responding to the crowds jeering as Germany underperformed against South Korea in the USA in 1990. His middle finger gesture saw him sent home in disgrace and he hasn't played for his country since!

But thankfully the Argentines were sent home with a taste of their own medicine when the lanky Dutch goalkeeper Van Der Saar berated the Argentines' star striker Ortega for a blatant dive and Ortega reacted with a head butt. Van Der Saar fell dramatically and the Argentine received his marching orders. Literally one minute later, Dennis Bergkamp scored the winning goal for Holland and the Argentinians were on their way home.

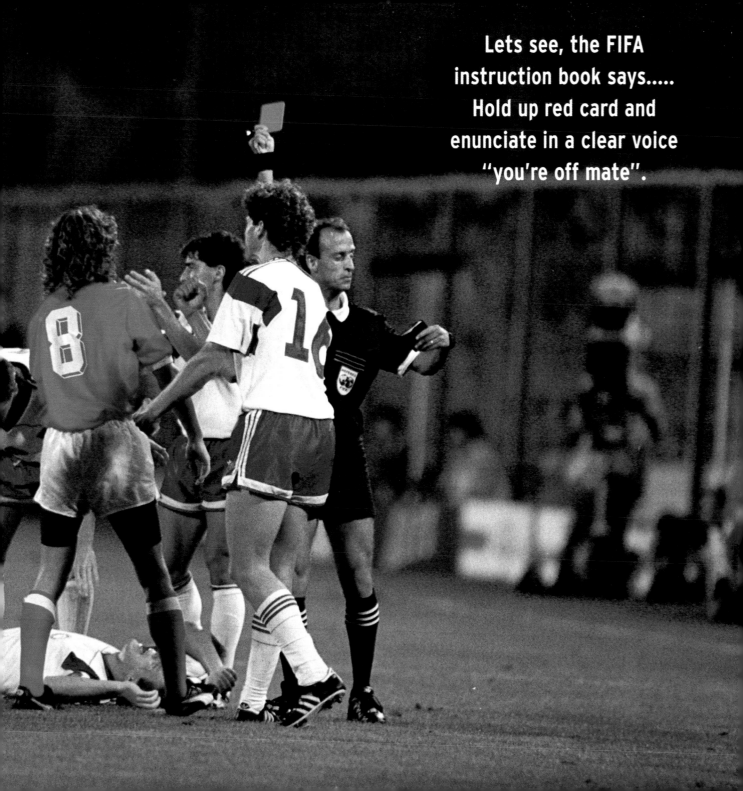

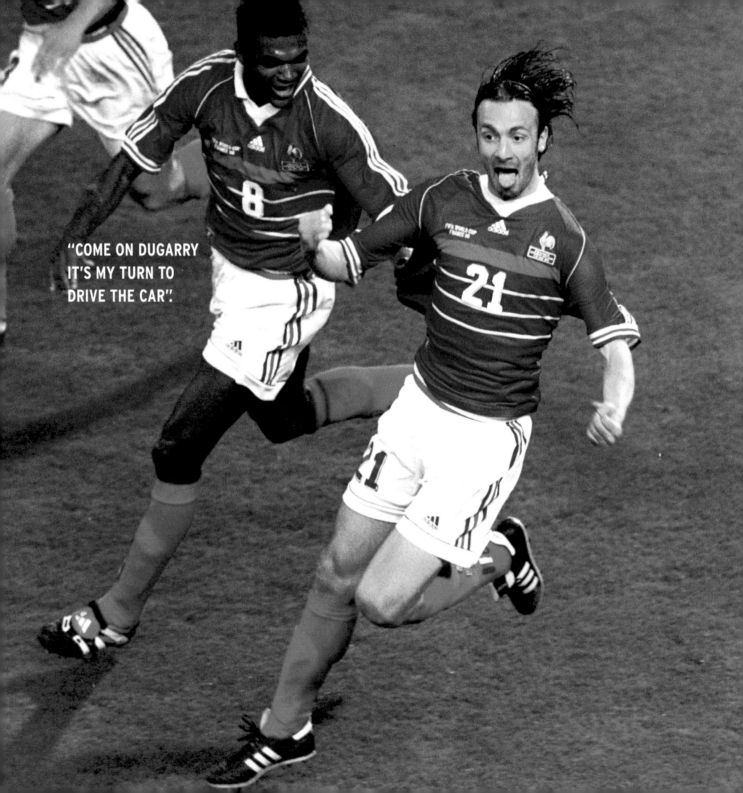

"COME ON DUGARRY
IT'S MY TURN TO
DRIVE THE CAR".

BUTTING IN FOR JUSTICE

England's last 16 match with Argentina in France '98 was one of the greatest matches seen in the World Cup. It will always be remembered though for David Beckham's sending off for petulant retaliation after a foul by Argentine captain Simeone, which led to the England star being sent off and ultimately defeat for the English. Simeone had fouled Beckham and then pushed his face into the turf and when Beckham lashed out Simeone hit the ground as if he'd been shot. His Inter Milan teammate Pagliuca, the Italy goalkeeper, remarked: "I know Simeone, he was play acting".

The Argentinians went on to face Holland in the quarter-final, where the Dutch defender Numan received marching orders for a foul on - guess who - Simeone. Again, when fouled, Simeone rolled about 20 yards in mock agony, to which Diego Maradona, commentating for a TV Station, remarked ; "He's a sly one. That's 2 he's got sent off now."

BATTLE *2 - SANTIAGO

Italy versus the hosts Chile in 1962 was always going to be a tense encounter. The South Americans were deeply offended by the Italians' habit of using the lure of the lire to poach players from their continent to play for Italy (still legal in those days), thus players who had appeared for Brazil and Argentina in 1958 played for Italy in Chile. To help matters along, two Italian journalists wrote incredibly damning articles about Chile, which were relayed back to the Chilean nation. To say this was a grudge match would be an understatement. The Chileans spent the whole match winding up the Italians with niggly fouls and spitting in their faces. The game, according to legendary British referee Ken Aston, was uncontrollable. Two Italians were sent off, one for a foul and one for aiming a kick at the head of the Chilean midfielder, Sanchez, who had earlier escaped punishment despite breaking an opponent's nose with a neat left hook!

PERU-VING A NUISANCE

Peruvian goalkeeper Quiroga caused a sensation in the 1978 finals in the match against Poland when he was booked for a foul - in his opponents half of the field!

RUUD GULLIT WITH A BAD HAIR DAY

"RUDI, YOU'VE GOT SOMETHING GREEN AND SLIMY IN YOUR HAIR."

"QUICK HIDE, I THINK THAT'S GAZZA OVER THERE."

Part of the romance of the World Cup is the competition's ability to throw up a shock or two. When you throw together so many teams for so many matches in such diverse conditions, the chances are that at least one unexpected result will occur. Throughout the history of the tournament there have been many notable and celebrated surprise packages. This chapter takes a look at the smaller nations that have charmed and astonished the watching millions.

ITALY-OH-NO

North Korea came to the finals in 1966 with little or no reputation. They had qualified simply by beating Australia and little was expected of them. When they lost their opening match 3-0 to Russia this seemed to confirm most people's suspicions. They were to play their matches at Ayresome Park, Middlesbrough, where the fans warmed to the neat, speedy Koreans and adopted them as their own. The Boro faithful were rewarded when the Koreans snatched a draw with Chile as their confidence grew.

The most famous moment in North Korea's footballing history came against Italy at Ayresome Park. A shock 1-0 victory sent the Italians home and led to a quarter-final with Portugal (featuring the mighty Eusebio) at Goodison Park. Half of Middlesbrough travelled to Liverpool to cheer the North Koreans on and were amazed to see their adopted side storm into a three goal lead in 25 minutes. In one of the other matches England faced Argentina, and during a pause in play, Roger Hunt pointed out this score to Gordon Banks. They agreed that it must have been a mistake!

"Chief big tits"

THE SHOT PUTTERS

The shock package in the first tournament in Uruguay 1930 was the powerfully built USA side. They muscled their way to 3-0 victories over both Belgium and Paraguay - their nickname - "The Shot Putters".

MILLA THRILLA

Cameroon illuminated the finals in 1990 and 1994. Defeating the champions, Argentina, in the opening match of Italia '90 marked their arrival on the scene and it was Roger Milla with his jiggly-hipped celebration that captured the hearts of the World. Milla holds the record for the oldest player to score in the finals (when he was supposedly 42 in 1994. Observers claim the striker was closer to 45!

The USA also provided a major surprise in Brazil in 1950 when they overturned England 1-0. This was England's first time in the tournament and much was expected of them, but a single goal from Joe Gaetjens was enough to leave them with egg on their faces. England's Wilf Mannion's much quoted response was "Can we play them again tommorow?"

NORTHERN LIGHTS

Teams from Northern Ireland have provided the World Cup with a number of fairy stories over the years. In 1958, when all four home countries qualified for the finals in Sweden, the Northern Ireland side made it all the way to the quarter-finals, even beating the mighty Czech side on the way. Being forced to play 5 games in 12 days did for the Irish in the end, and they were not to qualify again until Spain in 1982.

"NEVER MIND THE TICKET FIASCO, YOU COULD WAIT MONTHS FOR A DRINK."

"NO DAD, THE BALL'S ROUND LIKE THIS."

SCOT'S THE MATTER WITH THEM

Scotland have always had their problems with so called 'lesser teams' in the World Cup. In 1978 when they were so confident of victory, they drew with Iran, the Iranian's only World Cup point before France '98. In 1990 it was the turn of Costa Rica to defeat the Scots and in 1998, the Moroccans inflicted a 3-0 defeat on the Tartan Army. Most annoyingly for the Scotland fans, they always manage to do well against the better teams - in 1978, they beat the eventual runners up Holland 3-1, and in 1998 achieved a creditable draw with a talented Norway side.

An honourable mention must also go to Wales who nearly completed one of the shock results of all time in Sweden in 1958. They held Brazil at 0-0 for 73 minutes until they succumbed to Pele's first ever goal in the World Cup.

Roger Milla's most memorable goal came against Colombia when Colombia's scorpion-kicking keeper Rene Higuita decided to go on a bit of a dribble. Milla tackled him and ran the ball into the empty net leaving Higuita looking a little bit silly.

The Koreans couldn't hold on and were beaten 5-3, but they left with a new found respect and an unexpected hotel bill; fully expecting to be eliminated, they had only booked accommodation for the first round matches!

Norman Whiteside became the youngest player to appear in the World Cup Finals when he pulled on an Northern Ireland shirt for the match with Yugoslavia aged 17 years and 41 days. The team's performances in this tournament will never be forgotten, forcing a creditable draw with Austria and amazingly overturning the hosts Spain 1-0 with ten men. As in 1958, the Northern Irish were beaten by France in the quarter-finals.

"OK GUYS - I'VE READ THE WHOLE SOCCER RULE BOOK, AND THERE'S NOTHING THAT SAYS WE CAN'T KEEP THE BALL LIKE THIS, NOW SHUT-UP AND START WALKING TOWARDS GOAL."

NICE FANS, NICE TEAM, VERY TIDY, VERY NICE...

...BUT DON'T ASK FOR AN APOLOGY

THE GOOD

THE BAD

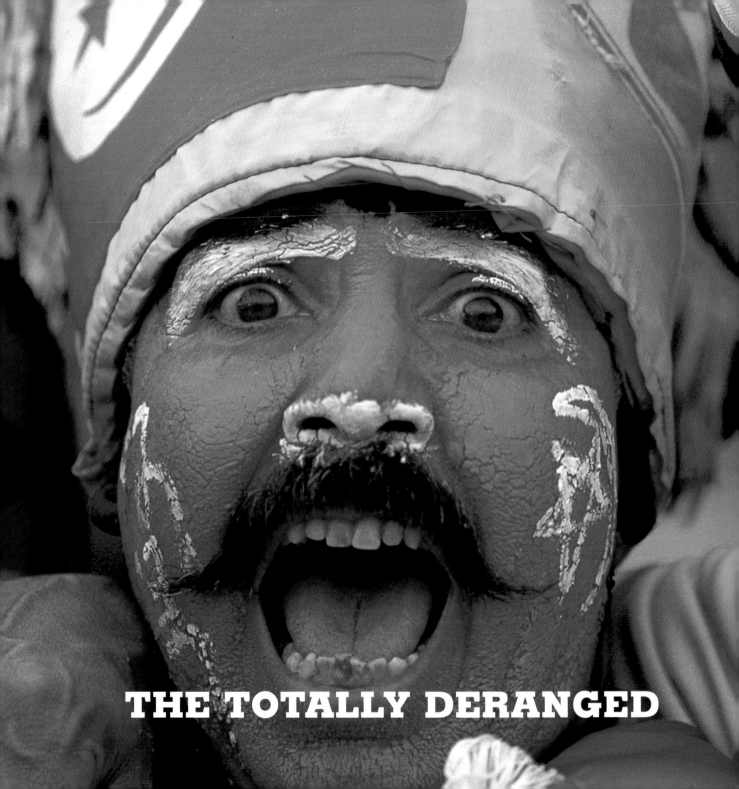

THE TOTALLY DERANGED

AND THE ABSOLUTELY
TOTALLY DERANGED!

"THE DUTCH THEY'RE
SO WACKY".

HE'S GOT THE HORN

THE FRENCH MERCHANDISE
DIDN'T SELL AS WELL AS
EXPECTED.

A TYPICAL JAMAICAN
FAN

A TYPICAL
ENGLISH FAN

HE'S MAD!

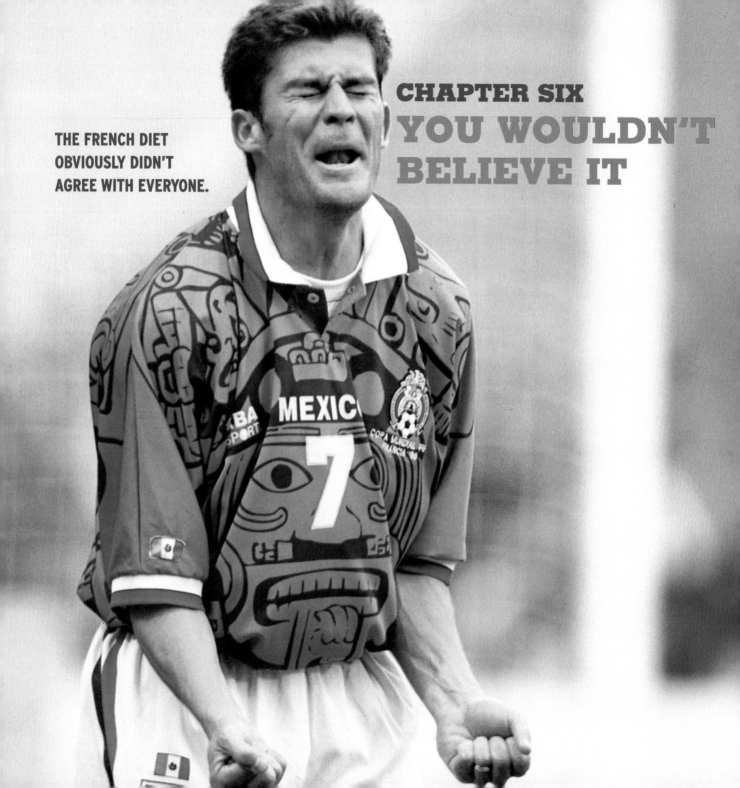

THE FRENCH DIET
OBVIOUSLY DIDN'T
AGREE WITH EVERYONE.

CHAPTER SIX
YOU WOULDN'T
BELIEVE IT

BLONDES HAVE MORE FUN

Hair dye was the craze amongst players during France '98. Croatia's Boban had his country's colours dyed into the back of his head and Scotland's Craig Burley dyed his hair blonde in celebration of his goal against Norway. The Scots also pledged to dye their hair if they went through to the second round, but they failed. Shame really, as albino Colin Hendry had promised to dye his hair black! Stars of the show though were The Romanian Team, who did qualify and did dye their hair. All of them - blonde. And, yes, they looked ridiculous. By the way, they lost their next match.

CHINESE WHISPERS

London's telephone network was alive with excited voices as a vicious rumour spread throughout the city two days after England's defeat by Argentina. The rumour was that Argentina had been kicked out of the World Cup after 3 players failed drug tests. Unfortunately, the rumour turned out to be false, having emerged on the internet somewhere in the City of London. Still, it gave us all some hope for a couple of hours.

HE'S GOT HIS HEAD UP
HIS ARSE.

DENIS BERGKAMP'S
EFFORTS TO BEAT HIS
FEAR OF FLYING WERE
ALWAYS DOOMED TO
FAILURE.

"WHAT'S WRONG, ALAN, I ONLY
SAID, AH WELL, IT'S ONLY A GAME".

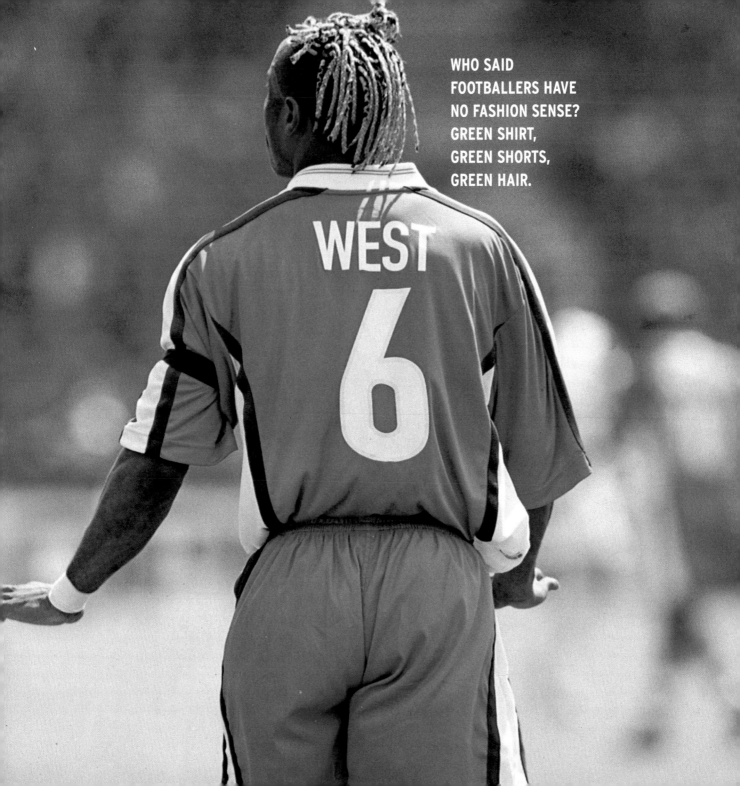

WHO SAID FOOTBALLERS HAVE NO FASHION SENSE? GREEN SHIRT, GREEN SHORTS, GREEN HAIR.

"GIVE ME BACK MY TEETH."

THE MOST ATTRACTIVE
FACE OF SCOTTISH
FOOTBALL.

"PLEASE GIVE US OUR TROPHY BACK."

UNDER THE THUMB

Andreas Moller, the German midfielder, has had a torrid time with the German coach Bertie Vogts during France '98. Substituted for the first two matches and on the bench for the second two, his sulking became pronounced after a call from his wife urging him to come home. The reason? During one match she had been sitting behind the German bench where she had heard Vogts repeatedly abusing her husband. He foolishly announced this to the press and spent the next match with his arse firmly on the bench. Unfortunately, Germany were knocked out and it looks like Moller's World Cup career is over. Our hearts bleed.

THAT'LL TEACH THEM

The two coaches who must have wished they'd kept their opinions to themselves during France '98 must be Aime Jacquet of France and Berti Vogts of Germany. Jacquet had called for 'more discipline' from referees in the tournament before his side's match with South Korea. Unfortunately for him his wishes came true and star player Zinedine Zidane was sent off for stamping on an opponent. Similarly, Berti Vogts called for the referee to control Germany's quarter-final with Croatia extremely carefully following their ill-tempered clash during Euro '96. The referee was extremely strict and a German defender,   was sent off in the first half, allowing Croatia to win 3-0, sending the ageing Germans back home.

THE CURSE OF ADIDAS

The money men at Adidas must have been kicking themselves by the end of France '98. Their chosen stars without exception had black marks on their tournaments. France's Zidane and Holland's Kluivert were both sent off during the first round, whilst Italy's Del Piero and England's Beckham were both left out for their teams' opening matches. Worst blunder of all was an advertisement which ran in the UK press the day of England's match versus Argentina. It carried a picture of David Beckham, and text which read "Tonight's match between England and Argentina will be remembered for what one man did with his feet." Indeed it was - Beckham was sent off for kicking out at the Argentinian captain Simeone. England lost on penalties.

MARADOPER

One of the sensations of USA 1994 was the return of Diego Maradona to the Argentinian side. At 34 his performances were electric and he seemed on fire, particularly following one goal where he ran to a TV camera and screamed energetically into the lens. Everyone wondered how he'd managed to overcome his fitness and personal problems. This was answered when he was forced to take a dope test and tested positively for 5 different strains of stimulant.

WATER MESS

Brazilian full back Branco has always been reknowned for his fertile imagination. But not even hardened supporters could have expected his outburst following a match with Argentina in Italia '90. Branco claimed that he drank from an Argentinian water bottle during the match and that it was drugged to affect his performance. Surely it wasn't that he was just crap?

KIT'S A BIT HOT

Scotland's team to face Uruguay in Switzerland in 1964 must have been a bit daunted by their task. It was not the South Americans they had to worry about but their own kits, which, inappropriately for a match to be played in 100 degrees heat, were long sleeved, woollen jerseys.

PAINED REACTION

World Cup USA '94 was opened at Chicago by the legendary Diana Ross. After performing a song she was given the simple task of scoring the first goal of the tournament into an empty goal from 6 yards. Obviously she had been training with the US national team - she missed.

TAKING HOSPITALITY A BIT TOO FAR

During the 1974 Tournament, the German hosts provided each squad with a luxury coach to transport them between stadia. When the company turned up to collect the coach which had been lent to Zaire, they were amazed to find that the coach had left and was heading straight for Africa!

IT'S A DOG'S LIFE

One famous incident from the 1962 finals occured during England's match with Brazil. England were 3-1 down in the second half when the game was stopped as a mongrel dog ran onto the pitch. Various players chased the mutt in an attempt to catch it but none were successful, until Jimmy Greaves managed to charm the dog into his arms. Unfortunately for Greaves, his clean white England jersey quickly developed a yellow patch as the animal urinated all over him. A strange twist to this tale is that the Brazilian star Garrincha decided to adopt the dog and Greaves became a folk hero in Brazil!

SOWING THE SEA-DS

Argentina 1978 was almost plunged into crisis when some of the pitches were foolishly watered with sea water - causing them to spoil almost instantly. Luckily the authorities were able to re-turf the pitches in time.

BOOTED OUT

The great Leonidas of Brazil caused a storm during the match with Poland in 1938 when, in order to cope with the weather conditions, he tried to remove his boots and play barefoot. The Swedish referee was not amused and ordered the striker to get his boots back on. Similarly upset were the India squad of 1950, who refused to participate after FIFA ruled that all teams would have to wear boots!

KING OF THE WORLD (CUP)

Romania's squad for the first tournament in Uruguay in 1930 was picked by none other than the ruler of the country, King Carol. He also persuaded all the companies that employed Romanian players to give them time off for the tournament.

NO SERIOUSLY...

O.K., lads. We've had the laughs -the fighting starts here! These are my ten greatest teams and ten greatest players. Simply drink ten pints of lager and discuss...

10 GREATEST PLAYERS

1 - Pele (Brazil)

2 - Maradona (Argentina)

3 - Cruyff (Holland)

4 - Puskas (Hungary)

5 - Garrincha (Brazil)

6 - Eusebio (Portugal)

7 - Beckenbauer (Germany)

8 - Rossi (Italy)

9 - Kempes (Argentina)

10 - Moore (England)

10 GREATEST TEAMS

1 - Brazil (Mexico '70)

2 - Brazil (Chile '62)

3 - Holland (Germany'74)

4 - Brazil (Sweden '58)

5 - England (England '66)

6 - Italy (Spain '82)

7 - Holland (Argentina '78)

8 - Germany (Italia '90)

9 - Hungary (Switzerland'54)

10 - Argentina(Argentina'78)

IF YOU ENJOYED THIS BOOK, WHAT ABOUT THESE!

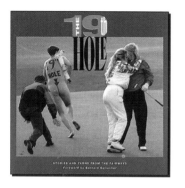

All these books are available at your local book shop or can be ordered direct from the publisher.

Just list the titles you require and give your name address, including postcode.

Prices and availability are subject to change without notice.

Please send to Chameleon Cash Sales, 76 Dean Street, London W1V 5HA, a cheque or postal order for £7.99 and add the following for postage and packaging:

UK - £1.00 For the first book, 50p for the second and 30p for the third and for each additional book up to a maximum of £3.00.

OVERSEAS - (including Eire) £2.00 For the first book, £1.00 for the second and 50p for each additional book up to a maximum of £3.00.